Stable Name:

_____

Stable Owner:

_____

Index

39

40.

41.

42.

43.

44.

45.

46.

47.

48.

49.

50.

51.

52.

53.

54.

55.

56.

57.

58.

59.

60.

61.

62

63.

64.

65.

66.

67.

68.

69.

70.

71.

72.

73.

74.

75.

76.

77.

78.

79.

80.

81.

82.

83.

84.

85.

86.

87.

88.

89.

90.

91.

92.

93.

94.

95.

96.

97.

98.

99.

100.

101.

102.

103.

104.

105.

106.

107.

108.

Name: _____

Mare / Stallion / Gelding	Date:
Breed:	Color:
Serial n°:	Year:
Brand:	Age:

Family members (+page):

Personality/other remarks:

Name: _____

Mare / Stallion / Gelding	Date:
Breed:	Color:
Serial n°:	Year:
Brand:	Age:

Family members (+page): _____

Personality/other remarks: _____

Name: _____

Mare / Stallion / Gelding	Date:
Breed:	Color:
Serial n°:	Year:
Brand:	Age:

Family members (+page):

Personality/other remarks:

Name: _____

Mare / Stallion / Gelding	Date:
Breed:	Color:
Serial n°:	Year:
Brand:	Age:

Family members (+page): _____

_____

Personality/other remarks: _____

_____

_____

_____

_____

_____

Name: _____

Mare / Stallion / Gelding	Date:
Breed:	Color:
Serial n°:	Year:
Brand:	Age:

Family members (+page):

Personality/other remarks:

Name: _____

Mare / Stallion / Gelding	Date:
Breed:	Color:
Serial n°:	Year:
Brand:	Age:

Family members (+page): _____

Personality/other remarks: _____

_____

_____

_____

_____

_____

Name: _____

Mare / Stallion / Gelding	Date:
Breed:	Color:
Serial n°:	Year:
Brand:	Age:

Family members (+page):

Personality/other remarks:

Name: _____

Mare / Stallion / Gelding	Date:
Breed:	Color:
Serial n°:	Year:
Brand:	Age:

Family members (+page): _____

Personality/other remarks: _____

Name: _____

Mare / Stallion / Gelding	Date:
Breed:	Color:
Serial n°:	Year:
Brand:	Age:

Family members (+page):

Personality/other remarks:

Name: _____

Mare / Stallion / Gelding	Date:
Breed:	Color:
Serial n°:	Year:
Brand:	Age:

Family members (+page): _____

Personality/other remarks: _____

_____

_____

_____

_____

Name: _____

Mare / Stallion / Gelding	Date:
Breed:	Color:
Serial n°:	Year:
Brand:	Age:

Family members (+page):

Personality/other remarks:

Name: _____

Mare / Stallion / Gelding	Date:
Breed:	Color:
Serial n°:	Year:
Brand:	Age:

Family members (+page): _____

Personality/other remarks: _____

_____

_____

_____

_____

Name: _____

Mare / Stallion / Gelding	Date:
Breed:	Color:
Serial n°:	Year:
Brand:	Age:

Family members (+page):

Personality/other remarks:

Name: _____

Mare / Stallion / Gelding	Date:
Breed:	Color:
Serial n°:	Year:
Brand:	Age:

Family members (+page): _____

Personality/other remarks: _____

Name: _____

Mare / Stallion / Gelding	Date:
Breed:	Color:
Serial n°:	Year:
Brand:	Age:

Family members (+page):

Personality/other remarks:

Name: _____

Mare / Stallion / Gelding	Date:
Breed:	Color:
Serial n°:	Year:
Brand:	Age:

Family members (+page): _____

Personality/other remarks: _____

Name: _____

Mare / Stallion / Gelding | Date:
Breed: | Color:
Serial n°: | Year:
Brand: | Age:

Family members (+page):

Personality/other remarks:

Name: _____

Mare / Stallion / Gelding	Date:
Breed:	Color:
Serial n°:	Year:
Brand:	Age:

Family members (+page):

Personality/other remarks:

Name: _____

Mare / Stallion / Gelding	Date:
Breed:	Color:
Serial n°:	Year:
Brand:	Age:

Family members (+page):

Personality/other remarks:

Name: _____

Mare / Stallion / Gelding | Date:
Breed: | Color:
Serial n°: | Year:
Brand: | Age:

Family members (+page): _____

Personality/other remarks: _____

_____

_____

_____

_____

_____

Name: _____

Mare / Stallion / Gelding	Date:
Breed:	Color:
Serial n°:	Year:
Brand:	Age:

Family members (+page):

Personality/other remarks:

Name: _____

Mare / Stallion / Gelding	Date:
Breed:	Color:
Serial n°:	Year:
Brand:	Age:

Family members (+page): _____

Personality/other remarks: _____

_____

_____

_____

_____

Name: _____

Mare / Stallion / Gelding	Date:
Breed:	Color:
Serial n°:	Year:
Brand:	Age:

Family members (+page):

Personality/other remarks:

Name: _____

Mare / Stallion / Gelding	Date:
Breed:	Color:
Serial n°:	Year:
Brand:	Age:

Family members (+page): _____

Personality/other remarks: _____

Name: _____

Mare / Stallion / Gelding	Date:
Breed:	Color:
Serial n°:	Year:
Brand:	Age:

Family members (+page):

Personality/other remarks:

Name: _____

Mare / Stallion / Gelding	Date:
Breed:	Color:
Serial n°:	Year:
Brand:	Age:

Family members (+page): _____

Personality/other remarks: _____

_____

_____

_____

_____

Name: _____

Mare / Stallion / Gelding	Date:
Breed:	Color:
Serial n°:	Year:
Brand:	Age:

Family members (+page):

Personality/other remarks:

Name: _____

Mare / Stallion / Gelding	Date:
Breed:	Color:
Serial n°:	Year:
Brand:	Age:

Family members (+page): _____

Personality/other remarks: _____

_____

_____

_____

_____

Name: _____

Mare / Stallion / Gelding | Date:
Breed: | Color:
Serial n°: | Year:
Brand: | Age:

Family members (+page):

Personality/other remarks:

Name: _____

Mare / Stallion / Gelding	Date:
Breed:	Color:
Serial n°:	Year:
Brand:	Age:

Family members (+page): _____

Personality/other remarks: _____

_____

_____

_____

_____

_____

_____

Name: _____

Mare / Stallion / Gelding	Date:
Breed:	Color:
Serial n°:	Year:
Brand:	Age:

Family members (+page):

Personality/other remarks:

Name: _____

Mare / Stallion / Gelding	Date:
Breed:	Color:
Serial n°:	Year:
Brand:	Age:

Family members (+page): _____

Personality/other remarks: _____

_____

_____

_____

_____

Name: _____

Mare / Stallion / Gelding	Date:
Breed:	Color:
Serial n°:	Year:
Brand:	Age:

Family members (+page):

Personality/other remarks:

Name: _____

Mare / Stallion / Gelding	Date:
Breed:	Color:
Serial n°:	Year:
Brand:	Age:

Family members (+page):

Personality/other remarks:

Name: _____

Mare / Stallion / Gelding	Date:
Breed:	Color:
Serial n°:	Year:
Brand:	Age:

Family members (+page):

_____

Personality/other remarks:

_____

_____

_____

_____

_____

Name: _____

Mare / Stallion / Gelding	Date:
Breed:	Color:
Serial n°:	Year:
Brand:	Age:

Family members (+page):

Personality/other remarks:

Name: _____

Mare / Stallion / Gelding	Date:
Breed:	Color:
Serial n°:	Year:
Brand:	Age:

Family members (+page):

Personality/other remarks:

Name: _____

Mare / Stallion / Gelding	Date:
Breed:	Color:
Serial n°:	Year:
Brand:	Age:

Family members (+page): _____

Personality/other remarks: _____

_____

_____

_____

_____

Name: _____

Mare / Stallion / Gelding	Date:
Breed:	Color:
Serial n°:	Year:
Brand:	Age:

Family members (+page):

Personality/other remarks:

Name: _____

Mare / Stallion / Gelding | Date:
Breed: | Color:
Serial n°: | Year:
Brand: | Age:

Family members (+page): _____

Personality/other remarks: _____

Name: _____

Mare / Stallion / Gelding	Date:
Breed:	Color:
Serial n°:	Year:
Brand:	Age:

Family members (+page): _____

Personality/other remarks: _____

Name: _____

Mare / Stallion / Gelding	Date:
Breed:	Color:
Serial n°:	Year:
Brand:	Age:

Family members (+page): _____

Personality/other remarks: _____

_____

_____

_____

_____

_____

Name: _____

Mare / Stallion / Gelding	Date:
Breed:	Color:
Serial n°:	Year:
Brand:	Age:

Family members (+page): _____

Personality/other remarks: _____

Name: _____

Mare / Stallion / Gelding	Date:
Breed:	Color:
Serial n°:	Year:
Brand:	Age:

Family members (+page): _____

Personality/other remarks: _____

_____

_____

_____

_____

_____

Name: _____

Mare / Stallion / Gelding | Date:
Breed: | Color:
Serial n°: | Year:
Brand: | Age:

Family members (+page):

Personality/other remarks:

Name: _____

Mare / Stallion / Gelding	Date:
Breed:	Color:
Serial n°:	Year:
Brand:	Age:

Family members (+page): _____

Personality/other remarks: _____

_____

_____

_____

_____

Name: _____

Mare / Stallion / Gelding	Date:
Breed:	Color:
Serial n°:	Year:
Brand:	Age:

Family members (+page):

Personality/other remarks:

Name: _____

Mare / Stallion / Gelding	Date:
Breed:	Color:
Serial n°:	Year:
Brand:	Age:

Family members (+page): _____

Personality/other remarks: _____

_____
_____
_____
_____

Name: _____

Mare / Stallion / Gelding	Date:
Breed:	Color:
Serial n°:	Year:
Brand:	Age:

Family members (+page):

Personality/other remarks:

Name: _____

Mare / Stallion / Gelding	Date:
Breed:	Color:
Serial n°:	Year:
Brand:	Age:

Family members (+page):

Personality/other remarks:

Name: _____

Mare / Stallion / Gelding	Date:
Breed:	Color:
Serial n°:	Year:
Brand:	Age:

Family members (+page):

Personality/other remarks:

Name: _____

Mare / Stallion / Gelding	Date:
Breed:	Color:
Serial n°:	Year:
Brand:	Age:

Family members (+page): _____

Personality/other remarks: _____

_____

_____

_____

_____

Name: _____

Mare / Stallion / Gelding	Date:
Breed:	Color:
Serial n°:	Year:
Brand:	Age:

Family members (+page):

Personality/other remarks:

Name: _____

Mare / Stallion / Gelding	Date:
Breed:	Color:
Serial n°:	Year:
Brand:	Age:

Family members (+page): _____

Personality/other remarks: _____

_____

_____

_____

_____

_____

Name: _____

Mare / Stallion / Gelding	Date:
Breed:	Color:
Serial n°:	Year:
Brand:	Age:

Family members (+page):

Personality/other remarks:

Name: _____

Mare / Stallion / Gelding	Date:
Breed:	Color:
Serial n°:	Year:
Brand:	Age:

Family members (+page): _____

Personality/other remarks: _____

Name: _____

Mare / Stallion / Gelding	Date:
Breed:	Color:
Serial n°:	Year:
Brand:	Age:

Family members (+page):

Personality/other remarks:

Name: _____

Mare / Stallion / Gelding	Date:
Breed:	Color:
Serial n°:	Year:
Brand:	Age:

Family members (+page): _____

Personality/other remarks: _____

_____

_____

_____

_____

Name: _____

Mare / Stallion / Gelding	Date:
Breed:	Color:
Serial n°:	Year:
Brand:	Age:

Family members (+page):

Personality/other remarks:

Name: _____

Mare / Stallion / Gelding	Date:
Breed:	Color:
Serial n°:	Year:
Brand:	Age:

Family members (+page): _____

Personality/other remarks: _____

_____

_____

_____

_____

Name: _____

Mare / Stallion / Gelding	Date:
Breed:	Color:
Serial n°:	Year:
Brand:	Age:

Family members (+page): _____

Personality/other remarks: _____

_____

_____

_____

_____

_____

Name: _____

Mare / Stallion / Gelding	Date:
Breed:	Color:
Serial n°:	Year:
Brand:	Age:

Family members (+page):

Personality/other remarks:

Name: _____

Mare / Stallion / Gelding	Date:
Breed:	Color:
Serial n°:	Year:
Brand:	Age:

Family members (+page):

Personality/other remarks:

Name: _____

Mare / Stallion / Gelding	Date:
Breed:	Color:
Serial n°:	Year:
Brand:	Age:

Family members (+page): _____

_____

Personality/other remarks: _____

_____

_____

_____

_____

_____

Name: _____

Mare / Stallion / Gelding	Date:
Breed:	Color:
Serial n°:	Year:
Brand:	Age:

Family members (+page):

Personality/other remarks:

Name: _____

Mare / Stallion / Gelding	Date:
Breed:	Color:
Serial n°:	Year:
Brand:	Age:

Family members (+page): _____

Personality/other remarks: _____

Name: _____

Mare / Stallion / Gelding	Date:
Breed:	Color:
Serial n°:	Year:
Brand:	Age:

Family members (+page): _____

_____

Personality/other remarks: _____

_____

_____

_____

_____

Name: _____

Mare / Stallion / Gelding	Date:
Breed:	Color:
Serial n°:	Year:
Brand:	Age:

Family members (+page): _____

Personality/other remarks: _____

_____

_____

_____

_____

Name: _____

Mare / Stallion / Gelding	Date:
Breed:	Color:
Serial n°:	Year:
Brand:	Age:

Family members (+page):

Personality/other remarks:

Name: _____

Mare / Stallion / Gelding	Date:
Breed:	Color:
Serial n°:	Year:
Brand:	Age:

Family members (+page): _____

Personality/other remarks: _____

_____
_____
_____
_____
_____

Name: _____

Mare / Stallion / Gelding	Date:
Breed:	Color:
Serial n°:	Year:
Brand:	Age:

Family members (+page):

Personality/other remarks:

Name: _____

Mare / Stallion / Gelding	Date:
Breed:	Color:
Serial n°:	Year:
Brand:	Age:

Family members (+page): _____

Personality/other remarks: _____

_____

_____

_____

_____

Name: _____

Mare / Stallion / Gelding	Date:
Breed:	Color:
Serial n°:	Year:
Brand:	Age:

Family members (+page): _____

_____

Personality/other remarks: _____

_____

_____

_____

_____

_____

Name: _____

Mare / Stallion / Gelding	Date:
Breed:	Color:
Serial n°:	Year:
Brand:	Age:

Family members (+page): _____

Personality/other remarks: _____

Name: _____

Mare / Stallion / Gelding | Date:
Breed: | Color:
Serial n°: | Year:
Brand: | Age:

Family members (+page):

Personality/other remarks:

Name: _____

Mare / Stallion / Gelding	Date:
Breed:	Color:
Serial n°:	Year:
Brand:	Age:

Family members (+page): _____

Personality/other remarks: _____

_____

_____

_____

_____

Name: _____

Mare / Stallion / Gelding	Date:
Breed:	Color:
Serial n°:	Year:
Brand:	Age:

Family members (+page):

Personality/other remarks:

Name: _____

Mare / Stallion / Gelding | Date:
Breed: | Color:
Serial n°: | Year:
Brand: | Age:

Family members (+page):

Personality/other remarks:

Name: _____

Mare / Stallion / Gelding	Date:
Breed:	Color:
Serial n°:	Year:
Brand:	Age:

Family members (+page):

_____

Personality/other remarks:

_____

_____

_____

_____

Name: _____

Mare / Stallion / Gelding	Date:
Breed:	Color:
Serial n°:	Year:
Brand:	Age:

Family members (+page): _____

Personality/other remarks: _____

_____

_____

_____

_____

Name: _____

Mare / Stallion / Gelding	Date:
Breed:	Color:
Serial n°:	Year:
Brand:	Age:

Family members (+page):

Personality/other remarks:

Name: _____

Mare / Stallion / Gelding	Date:
Breed:	Color:
Serial n°:	Year:
Brand:	Age:

Family members (+page): _____

Personality/other remarks: _____

_____

_____

_____

_____

Name: _____

Mare / Stallion / Gelding	Date:
Breed:	Color:
Serial n°:	Year:
Brand:	Age:

Family members (+page): _____

Personality/other remarks: _____

Name: _____

Mare / Stallion / Gelding	Date:
Breed:	Color:
Serial n°:	Year:
Brand:	Age:

Family members (+page):

Personality/other remarks:

Name: _____

Mare / Stallion / Gelding | Date:
Breed: | Color:
Serial n°: | Year:
Brand: | Age:

Family members (+page):

Personality/other remarks:

Name: _____

Mare / Stallion / Gelding	Date:
Breed:	Color:
Serial n°:	Year:
Brand:	Age:

Family members (+page): _____

Personality/other remarks: _____
_____
_____
_____
_____

Name: _____

Mare / Stallion / Gelding	Date:
Breed:	Color:
Serial n°:	Year:
Brand:	Age:

Family members (+page):

Personality/other remarks:

Name: _____

Mare / Stallion / Gelding	Date:
Breed:	Color:
Serial n°:	Year:
Brand:	Age:

Family members (+page): _____

Personality/other remarks: _____

_____

_____

_____

_____

Name: _____

Mare / Stallion / Gelding	Date:
Breed:	Color:
Serial n°:	Year:
Brand:	Age:

Family members (+page):

Personality/other remarks:

Name: _____

Mare / Stallion / Gelding	Date:
Breed:	Color:
Serial n°:	Year:
Brand:	Age:

Family members (+page): _____

Personality/other remarks: _____

_____

_____

_____

_____

Name: _____

Mare / Stallion / Gelding	Date:
Breed:	Color:
Serial n°:	Year:
Brand:	Age:

Family members (+page):

Personality/other remarks:

Name: _____

Mare / Stallion / Gelding	Date:
Breed:	Color:
Serial n°:	Year:
Brand:	Age:

Family members (+page):
_____

Personality/other remarks:
_____
_____
_____
_____
_____

Name: _____

Mare / Stallion / Gelding	Date:
Breed:	Color:
Serial n°:	Year:
Brand:	Age:

Family members (+page):

Personality/other remarks:

Name: _____

Mare / Stallion / Gelding	Date:
Breed:	Color:
Serial n°:	Year:
Brand:	Age:

Family members (+page): _____

Personality/other remarks: _____

_____

_____

_____

_____

Name: _____

Mare / Stallion / Gelding	Date:
Breed:	Color:
Serial n°:	Year:
Brand:	Age:

Family members (+page):

Personality/other remarks:

Name: _____

Mare / Stallion / Gelding | Date:
Breed: | Color:
Serial n°: | Year:
Brand: | Age:

Family members (+page): _____

Personality/other remarks: _____

Name: _____

Mare / Stallion / Gelding	Date:
Breed:	Color:
Serial n°:	Year:
Brand:	Age:

Family members (+page):
_____

Personality/other remarks:
_____
_____
_____
_____
_____

Name: _____

Mare / Stallion / Gelding	Date:
Breed:	Color:
Serial n°:	Year:
Brand:	Age:

Family members (+page):

Personality/other remarks:

Name: _____

Mare / Stallion / Gelding	Date:
Breed:	Color:
Serial n°:	Year:
Brand:	Age:

Family members (+page):

Personality/other remarks:

Name: _____

Mare / Stallion / Gelding	Date:
Breed:	Color:
Serial n°:	Year:
Brand:	Age:

Family members (+page): _____

Personality/other remarks: _____

_____

_____

_____

_____

Name: _____

Mare / Stallion / Gelding	Date:
Breed:	Color:
Serial n°:	Year:
Brand:	Age:

Family members (+page):

Personality/other remarks:

Name: _____

Mare / Stallion / Gelding	Date:
Breed:	Color:
Serial n°:	Year:
Brand:	Age:

Family members (+page): _____

Personality/other remarks: _____

Name: _____

Mare / Stallion / Gelding	Date:
Breed:	Color:
Serial n°:	Year:
Brand:	Age:

Family members (+page):

Personality/other remarks:

Wish List

1.
2.
3.
4.
5.
6.
7.
8.
9.
10.
11.
12.
13.
14.
15.
16.
17.
18.
19.
20.
21.
22.
23.
24.
25.
26.
27.
28.
29.
30.